THE FINANCIAL PLANNING WORKBOOK

A FAMILY BUDGETING GUIDE

LARRY BURKETT

MOODY PRESS

CHICAGO

© 1979, 1990, by
CHRISTIAN FINANCIAL CONCEPTS

Revised Edition, 1990

Library of Congress Cataloging in Publication Data

Burkett, Larry.
  The financial planning workbook.

  1. Finance, Personal.   2. Budgets, Personal.
3. Finance, Personal—Religious aspects—
Christianity.   I. Title.
HG179.B835   1982   332.024   82-7877
ISBN 0-8024-2545-3   AACR2

19 20 18

Printed in the United States of America

CONTENTS

INTRODUCTION

To many people, the word *budgeting* has a bad ring. Why? Because they see budgeting as a punishment plan. Unfortunately, this has often been the case with many families attempting to correct in one day financial problems that have been developing for several years.

It does not have to be so; a budget is simply a financial plan for the home. What is proposed in this workbook is a simple, workable plan for home money management; one that brings the financial area under God's control and relieves the burdens of worry, frustration, and anxiety. It maximizes family finances so that we are more effective for God both spiritually and financially. From this foundation the budget becomes a tool for good communications in an area normally characterized by conflict.

This workbook has been thoroughly tested as a tool to help families manage their finances. It is used in budget workshop seminars taught by Christian Financial Concepts, Inc. Video and audio tapes and instructor manuals are available for those who would like to teach this material in their communities. For further information, or to receive our monthly newsletter, contact Christian Financial Concepts, P.O. Box 2377, Gainesville, GA 30503-2377.

We are grateful to Mrs. Dianna Helms for her efforts in developing this workbook.

Getting Started

GETTING STARTED

THE GOAL — LIVING WITHIN OUR MEANS

WHAT DOES THIS MEAN?

It means to spend no more than we make on a monthly basis. Ideally that means to live on a cash basis and not use credit or borrowed money to provide normal living expenses. It also means the self-discipline to control spending and keep needs, wants, and desires in their proper relationship.

NEEDS	WANTS	DESIRES
These are the purchases necessary to provide your basic requirements such as food, clothing, home, medical coverage, and others (1 Timothy 6:8).	Wants involve choices about the quality of goods to be used. Dress clothes vs. work clothes, steak vs. hamburger, a new car vs. a used car, etc. 1 Peter 3:3-4 gives a point of reference for determining wants in a Christian's life.	These are choices according to God's plan that can be made only out of surplus funds after all other obligations have been met (1 John 2:15-16).

OBSTACLES TO GOOD PLANNING

Social pressures to own more "things."

The attitude that "more is better" regardless of the cost.

The use of credit to delay necessary decisions.

No surplus available to cope with rising prices and unexpected expenses.

We tend to offset increases in income by increasing our level of spending. That spending attitude is a real problem because it leads to:

THE DANGER POINT

When income barely equals outgo.

Break-even is not a *living point* but a *decision point*. If all the income is consumed in monthly expenses and something unusual happens, such as the family automobile breaking down, the result is additional indebtedness.

A decision is necessary at this point: *MAKE MORE MONEY OR SPEND LESS.*

Ideally this decision would be made before external pressures left few alternatives. Unfortunately when the pressure comes on, the credit card comes out. The result is a debt that cannot be paid. That limits the alternatives to treating the "symptoms." Some typical treatments are: bill consolidation loans, additional credit, second mortgages, or a job for the wife. Those may provide temporary relief. But, unfortunately, since only the symptom has been treated, the problem still exists. It's only a matter of time until the symptoms reappear.

It is obviously better to cut expenses than to attempt to increase income. Unfortunately, it is also painful. The key? *Commitment*.

RECOGNIZE THE DIVISIONS OF INCOME
(figure 1.1)

The *first* part belongs to God. It is returned to Him as a tithe in recognition that He owns all that we have. We are merely stewards.

> Will a man rob God? Yet you are robbing me! but you say, "How have
> we robbed Thee?" In tithes and contributions.
>
> Malachi 3:8

The *government* wants its share.

> Then He said to them, "Then render to Caesar the things that are Caesar's
> and to God the things that are God's."
>
> Matthew 22:21

The portion available after tithe and taxes is termed *net spendable income*.

Family needs come next.

> But if anyone does not provide for his own, and especially for those of his
> household, he has denied the faith, and is worse than an unbeliever.
>
> 1 Timothy 5:8

God says pay your *debts*.

> The wicked borrows and does not pay back, but the righteous is gracious
> and gives.
>
> Psalm 37:21

Faithful management will yield a fifth portion.

The creation of a *surplus* should be a major goal for the Christian. It is the surplus that allows us to respond to the needs of others.

> At this present time your abundance being a supply for their want, that
> their abundance also may become a supply for your want, that there may
> be equality.
>
> 2 Corinthians 8:14

Even if a family is not in debt, their finances should be budget controlled to maximize the surplus.

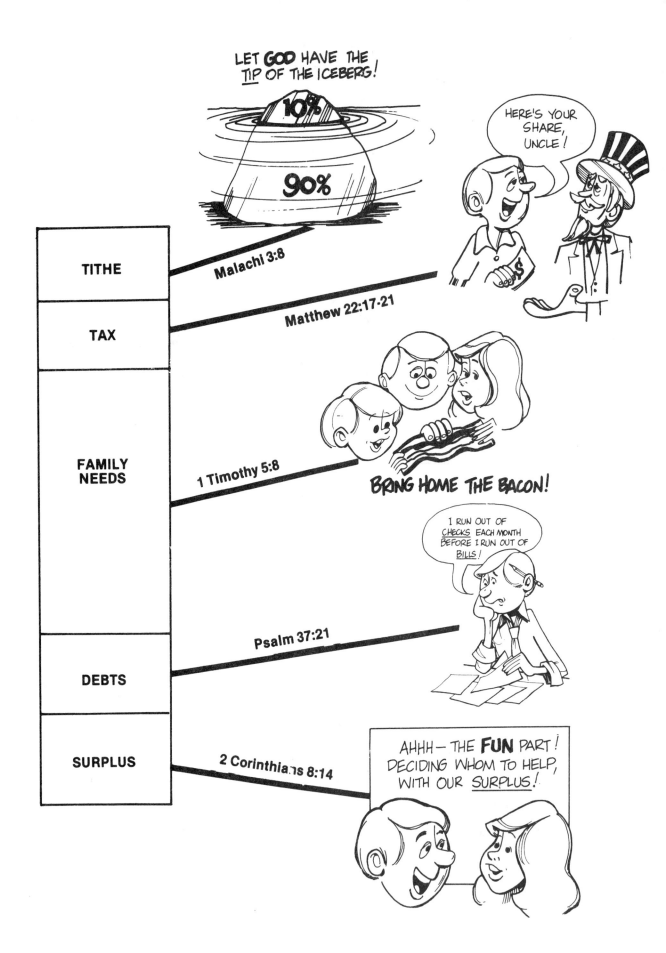

Figure 1.1

In addition to responding to the needs of others, it's the surplus that provides the flexibility to meet emergencies without credit. That surplus can also be used to invest and multiply your assets.

WHERE DO WE START?

Starting a budget is just like starting on a trip. You cannot set a course without first determining where you are.

Step one — The budget: What is the present level of spending?

Step two — Budget goals: Establish the "ideal" budget. In actuality, few people ever reach the ideal. But it is possible to establish the "now" condition by reviewing the ideal.

In establishing a budget this trip will consist of comparing the present spending level with a guideline for balanced spending. The comparison will point out where adjustments should be made.

Once the budget is established, a control system must be incorporated that will keep spending on the "road." The system must be able to sound the alarm *before* overspending occurs.

THERE ARE ROAD HAZARDS

DISCOURAGEMENT:

To complete the trip one must keep going. A major problem is to develop a budget and then *not* follow it.

LEGALISM:

Another problem is becoming legalistic and inflexible. Then the budget becomes a family weapon instead of a family tool. Becoming legalistic, incidentally, seems to occur at the same time the money runs out. If a road is blocked we usually have to take another route to get where we are going. Remain flexible to necessary changes.

OVERCORRECTION:

When the money gets tight, the tendency is to eliminate clothes, entertainment, food, and other "expendables." That creates a pressure that is often relieved by overspending in other areas.

EVERYBODY NEEDS A BUDGET!

Financial bondage can result from a lack of money and overspending. But it can also be caused from the misuse of an abundance of money. Some families have enough money to be undisciplined and get away with it (financially speaking). But true financial freedom requires that we be good stewards (Matthew 24:45). That is only possible with self-discipline.

A good plan requires *action* and *discipline* to make it work.

It may require sacrifice.

Begin *now!*

SECTION 2
Where Are We?

DETERMINING MONTHLY INCOME AND EXPENSES

THE PRESENT CONDITION

On the monthly Income and Expenses form (figure 2.1 on page 15) compare actual monthly expenses with monthly income to determine present spending. (Note: You may need to keep a diary of expenses for a few months before you can accurately determine actual monthly expenses.)

To determine living cost, consider what represents a reasonable standard of living at your present income level. Reasonable, *not total*, sacrifices are necessary.

Therefore, when you set up your budget, include a reasonable amount for personal spending, e.g., clothes, savings, entertainment, recreation.

DETERMINING INCOME PER MONTH

NOTE: Use form 1 (Monthly Income and Expenses Sheet) for this section.

List all gross income (income before deductions) in the "Income Per Month" section on the Monthly Income and Expenses Sheet. Don't forget to include **commissions, bonuses, tips, and interest earned** that will be received over the next 12 months.

When income consists totally or partially of commissions or other fluctuating sources, average it for a year and divide by twelve. Use a low yearly average, not a high average.

If you are paid on a weekly or bi-weekly basis, take the total yearly income and divide by twelve.

Business expense reimbursements should not be considered family income. Avoid the trap of using expense money to buffer family spending or the result will be an indebtedness that cannot be paid.

WHAT IS "NET SPENDABLE INCOME"?

Net spendable income is that portion available for family spending. Some of your income does not belong to the family and therefore cannot be spent. For instance:

CATEGORY 1 — **The Tithe:** Since the term *tithe* means "a tenth," I will assume that you give 10 percent of your total income to God. For a detailed discussion on the tithe, see *Your Finances in Changing Times* by Larry Burkett, published by Moody Press; chapter 10, "Sharing—God's Way."

CATEGORY 2 — **Taxes:** Federal withholding, social security, and state and local taxes must also be deducted from gross income. Self-employed individuals must not forget to set aside money for quarterly prepayments on taxes. Beware of the tendency to treat unpaid tax money as windfall profit.

Other Deductions: Payroll deductions for insurance, credit union savings or debt payments, bonds, stock programs, retirement, and union dues can be handled in either of two ways.

1. Treat them as a deduction from gross income the same as the income taxes.

2. Include them in spendable income and deduct them from the proper category. This is preferred because it provides a more accurate picture of where the money is being spent.

NET SPENDABLE INCOME = GROSS INCOME MINUS TITHE AND MINUS TAXES.

HOW IS NET SPENDABLE INCOME BEING SPENT?

CATEGORY 3 — **Housing Expenses:** All monthly expenses necessary to operate the home, including taxes, insurance, maintenance, and utilities. The amount used for utility payments should be an average monthly amount for the past twelve months.

If you cannot establish an accurate maintenance expense, use 5 percent of the monthly mortgage payment.

CATEGORY 4 — **Food Expenses:** All grocery expenses, including paper goods and non-food products normally purchased at grocery stores. Include milk, bread, and items purchased in addition to regular shopping trips. *Do not include* eating out and daily lunches eaten away from home.

If you do not know your actual food expenses, keep a detailed spending record for 30 to 45 days.

CATEGORY 5 — **Automobile Expenses:** Includes payments, insurance, gas, oil, maintenance, depreciation, etc.

Depreciation is actually the money set aside to repair or replace the automobile. The minimum amount set aside should be sufficient to keep the car in decent repair and to replace it at least every four to five years.

If replacement funds are not available in the budget, the minimum allocation should be maintenance costs. Annual or semi-annual auto insurance payments should be set aside on a monthly basis, thereby avoiding the crisis of a neglected expense.

CATEGORY 6 — **Insurance:** Includes all insurance, such as health, life and disability, not associated with the home or auto.

CATEGORY 7 — **Debts:** Includes all monthly payments required to meet debt obligations. Home mortgage and automobile payments are not included here.

CATEGORY 8 — **Entertainment and Recreation:** Vacation savings, camping trips, club dues, sporting equipment, hobby expenses, and athletic events. Don't forget Little League expense, booster clubs, and so on.

CATEGORY 9 — **Clothing:** The average annual amount spent on clothes divided by 12. The minimum amount should be at least $10 per month per family member.

CATEGORY 10 — **Savings:** Every family should allocate something for savings. A savings account can provide funds for emergencies and is a key element in good planning and financial freedom.

CATEGORY 11 — **Medical Expenses:** Insurance deductibles, doctors' bills, eye glasses, drugs, orthodontist visits, etc. Use a yearly average divided by 12 to determine a monthly amount.

CATEGORY 12 — **Miscellaneous:** Specific expenses that do not seem to fit anywhere else; pocket allowance (coffee money), miscellaneous gifts, Christmas presents, toiletries, haircuts, etc.

Miscellaneous spending is usually underestimated. A 30- to 45-day spending record is usually necessary to establish accurate present spending habits. Self-discipline is the key to controlling miscellaneous spending.

CATEGORY 13 — **School/Child Care:** An ever increasing segment of our population has expenses for private school and/or child care. This category must reflect those expenses. All other categories must be reduced to provide these funds.

CATEGORY 14 — **Investments:** Individuals and families with surplus income in their budgets will have the opportunity to invest for retirement or other long-term goals. As debt-free status is achieved, more money can be diverted to this category.

UNALLOCATED SURPLUS INCOME

CATEGORY 15 — **Unallocated Surplus Income:** Income from unbudgeted sources (garage sales, gifts, etc.) can be kept in one's checking account and placed in this category. This section can be useful to keep track of surplus income as well as to keep records for tax purposes. See page 41.

INCOME VS. EXPENSES

STEP ONE: Compile the expenses under each of the major categories (items 3 through 12) and note this as the total expense. Then in the space provided, subtract expenses from net spendable income.

STEP TWO: *If income is greater than expenses,* you need only to control spending to maximize the surplus. Section 5 will help you to do this.

STEP THREE: *If expenses are greater than income,* a detailed analysis will be necessary to correct the situation and restore a proper balance. Proceed to the next section.

WHERE ARE YOU?

MONTHLY INCOME & EXPENSES

GROSS INCOME PER MONTH $2,083

Salary	2,083
Interest	
Dividends	
Other	

LESS:

1. **Tithe**   125

2. **Tax** (Est. - Incl. Fed., State, FICA)   500

NET SPENDABLE INCOME   1,458

3. **Housing**   573

Mortgage (rent)	423
Insurance	
Taxes	
Electricity	70
Gas	20
Water	10
Sanitation	
Telephone	30
Maintenance	20
Other	

4. **Food**   230

5. **Automobile(s)**   285

Payments	140
Gas & Oil	40
Insurance	60
License/Taxes	5
Maint./Repair/Replace	40

6. **Insurance**   39

Life	14
Medical	25
Other	

7. **Debts**   90

Credit Card	90
Loans & Notes	
Other	

8. **Enter. & Recreation**   100

Eating Out	35
Baby Sitters	
Activities/Trips	20
Vacation	10
Other	35

9. **Clothing**   50

10. **Savings**   0

11. **Medical Expenses**   20

Doctor	20
Dentist	
Drugs	
Other	

12. **Miscellaneous**   145

Toiletry, cosmetics	19
Beauty, barber	15
Laundry, cleaning	15
Allowances, lunches	16
Subscriptions	20
Gifts (incl. Christmas)	25
Cash	35
Other	

13. **School/Child Care**   0

Tuition	
Materials	
Transportation	
Day Care	

14. **Investments**   0

TOTAL EXPENSES   1,532

INCOME VS. EXPENSES

Net Spendable Income	1,458
Less Expenses	1,532
	−74

15. **Unallocated Surplus Income** [1]

---

[1] This category is used when surplus income is received. This would be kept in the checking account to be used within a few weeks; otherwise, it should be transferred to an allocated category. See page 41 for further information.

Figure 2.1

Short-Range Planning

HANDLING THE VARIABLES BY SHORT-RANGE PLANNING

WHAT IS SHORT-RANGE PLANNING?

Budgeting for irregular expenses on a monthly basis. That includes fluctuating utility bills, auto maintenance, medical expenses, clothing, etc. See figure 3.1.

EXAMPLE: 1. By averaging utility bills over one year, money can be stored from low use months to offset the cost of high use months.

2. Annual or semi-annual insurance payments are met by establishing a monthly reserve.

Expenditures for clothing and medical and dental bills are other examples for which provision should be made. Those items normally are not purchased on a regular basis. Without the needed reserves, the result is often additional debt when those purchases must be made.

A vacation can be planned the same way. Plan what is needed for the coming year's vacation and divide the amount by 12 to determine what must be saved on a monthly basis.

Items such as automobiles, appliances, and household goods (furniture, rugs, drapes, etc.) wear out or deteriorate over time. Periodic allocations should be made to replace those items as necessary.

Ideally, automobile depreciation and maintenance should be allocated on a monthly basis. That savings would then pay for maintenance, insurance, and replacement of the automobile (assuming the car is kept for five years or 100,000 miles).

A DANGER—The tendency in tight budgeting situations is to avoid maintenance and depreciation savings with the excuse that "we just can't afford it." Even if the full amount cannot be set aside, try to save something for those purposes. Depreciation is the same as any other expense. Without money to repair a car, the usual alternative is to replace it—on the time payment plan!

Failure to plan for short-range variables and depreciating items results in crisis planning. Control your expenditures; don't let them control you.

HOW TO DO THIS

Use the table illustrated in figure 3.2 (page 20) to determine how much must be allocated to the various categories. For example, if automobile insurance is $420 per year, set aside $35 per month so that the bill can be paid when due.

Include those amounts in the proper categories when planning the total budget (use form 2).

At the end of each month the allocated money not actually used is transferred to a savings account (illustrated in figure 3.1). The savings ledger shows the various categories for which money is being saved (form 6).

ESTABLISH ACCOUNT LIMITS. Each account should have a predetermined limit. Once that limit has been reached no additional savings are necessary.

EXAMPLE: Assume $600 is the yearly total for medical expenses. Once the savings for medical reaches $600, the needed reserve has been met. Unless greater medical expenses are expected, savings beyond $600 are not necessary. Monthly funds can then be applied elsewhere until a medical expense occurs that reduces the amount in savings.

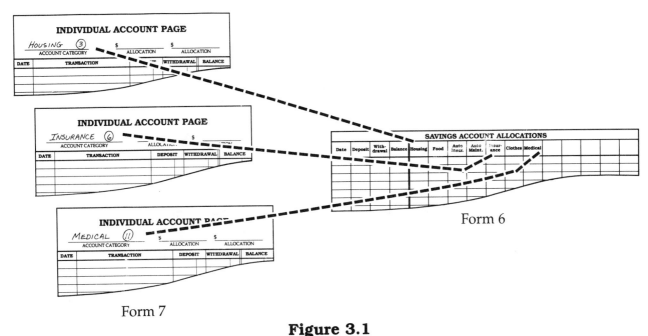

Form 7

Figure 3.1

Remember, the plan is to establish a reserve for variables, depreciating items, maintenance, or special needs such as fluctuating income. The savings account ledger divides the surplus by budget category.

BE FLEXIBLE. In starting a budget, it may be necessary to borrow from one account to supplement another. For example, if the car breaks down before a surplus is accumulated in the auto account, it may be necessary to borrow from the clothing or medical surpluses to pay for the car repair. However, to continue to do that month after month will defeat the long-range purpose in budgeting.

That purpose is to *plan ahead!*

	Estimated Cost	Per Month
1. VACATION	$ _____ ÷ 12 =	$ _____
2. DENTIST	$ _____ ÷ 12 =	$ _____
3. DOCTOR	$ __240__ ÷ 12 =	$ __20__
4. AUTOMOBILE	$ __480__ ÷ 12 =	$ __40__
5. ANNUAL INSURANCE	$ _____ ÷ 12 =	$ _____
(Life)	($ _____ ÷ 12 =	$ _____)
(Health)	($ _____ ÷ 12 =	$ _____)
(Auto)	($ __720__ ÷ 12 =	$ __60__)
(Home)	($ _____ ÷ 12 =	$ _____)
6. CLOTHING	$ __600__ ÷ 12 =	$ __50__
7. INVESTMENTS	$ _____ ÷ 12 =	$ _____
8. OTHER	$ _____ ÷ 12 =	$ _____
	$ _____ ÷ 12 =	$ _____

Figure 3.2

Budget Problems

BUDGET PROBLEM AREAS

BEWARE! Unforeseen problems can wreck your budget. Those include:

Bookkeeping Errors . . . Impulse Buying . . . Hidden Debts . . . Gifts

BOOKKEEPING ERRORS

An accurately balanced checkbook is a must. Even small errors result in big problems if they are allowed to compound. (A correct procedure is shown in Figure 4.1.)

An inaccurate balance can result in an overdrawn account, as well as in significant bank charges.

Automatic banking systems create additional pitfalls. Automatic payment deductions must be subtracted from the checkbook ledger at the time they are paid by the bank.

> EXAMPLE: An insurance premium is paid by automatic withdrawal on the fifteenth of each month. Since no statement or notice is received from the insurance company, you must make certain that on the fifteenth of every month the proper amount is deducted from your home checking account records.
>
> The same would be true for automatic credit card payments or any other automatic withdrawal.

Direct deposits into checking accounts must also be noted in the home ledger at the proper time. *Don't forget* to include bank service charges in the home ledger.

Automatic Tellers: If you withdraw cash from your account using an outside/automatic teller, be sure you write it in your ledger and file the transaction record.

OTHER FACTORS IN KEEPING GOOD RECORDS

1. *Use a ledger type checkbook rather than a stub type.* The ledger gives greater visibility and lends itself to fewer errors. I usually recommend using a checkbook that has a copy of the checks written. This eliminates errors in not posting a check.

2. *Make certain all checks are accounted for.* All checks should be entered in the ledger when written. This entry must include the check number, amount, date, and assignee.

Tearing checks out of your checkbook for future use defeats many of the safeguards built into this system. I recommend that all checks be written from the checkbook only.

3. *One bookkeeper only.* When more than one individual attempts to maintain the record system, confusion usually results. If the system is in good order, either the husband or the wife can keep the records. The choice should be based on who can do the job best. If the records are in a mess, the husband should assume the responsibility for correcting the situation.

4. *Maintain a home ledger.* If all records are kept in a checkbook ledger, you run the risk of losing it. A home ledger eliminates this possibility and makes record keeping more orderly. Form 7a is used as your checkbook ledger sheet. This will be explained in Section 7.

Checkbook Balance Procedure

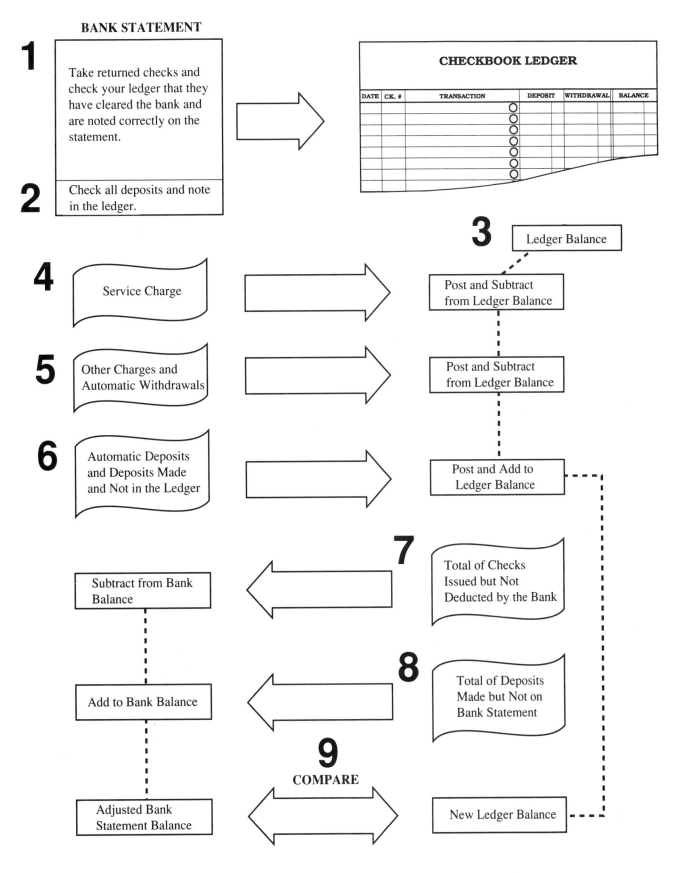

1 BANK STATEMENT — Take returned checks and check your ledger that they have cleared the bank and are noted correctly on the statement.

2 Check all deposits and note in the ledger.

CHECKBOOK LEDGER

DATE	CK. #	TRANSACTION	DEPOSIT	WITHDRAWAL	BALANCE

3 Ledger Balance

Post and Subtract from Ledger Balance

4 Service Charge → Post and Subtract from Ledger Balance

5 Other Charges and Automatic Withdrawals → Post and Subtract from Ledger Balance

6 Automatic Deposits and Deposits Made and Not in the Ledger → Post and Add to Ledger Balance

7 Total of Checks Issued but Not Deducted by the Bank → Subtract from Bank Balance

8 Total of Deposits Made but Not on Bank Statement → Add to Bank Balance

9 COMPARE

Adjusted Bank Statement Balance ↔ New Ledger Balance

Figure 4.1

5. *Balance the account—every month—to the penny.* Never allow the home ledger and bank statement to disagree in balance. The two most common errors are arithmetic errors (addition or subtraction) and transposition errors (writing in the wrong amount). Use a calculator and balance the account *to the penny.*

HIDDEN DEBTS

A common error is to overlook non-monthly debts such as doctor bills, family loans, bank notes, etc. Thus, when payments come due, there is no budget allocation for them.

To avoid surprises, establish and maintain a list of debts in total. The list must be reviewed and revised on a periodic basis, and the budget must anticipate necessary payments.

The list should reflect progress made on debt payments and can serve as a "payoff goal" sheet. Begin with a goal of eliminating the smallest debt first. Then double up on the next debt, and so on until all debts are eliminated.

Form 8 in the forms section is provided to list all outstanding debts. A copy is shown in figure 4.2. Note that space is provided for the name and number of the person to contact in the event of a problem.

IMPULSE BUYING

Impulse items are unnecessary purchases made on the spur-of-the-moment.

These purchases are usually rationalized by, "It was on sale," "I was planning to buy it anyway," "I've always wanted one," "I just couldn't resist it," or, "I owe it to myself." Often they are made with a credit card because the cash isn't available. The net result is a little-used item and an unnecessary debt.

"Impulse purchases" are not restricted to small items. They range from homes, cars, and trips to unscheduled luncheons. Cost is not the issue; necessity is. Every purchase should be considered in light of the budget.

Discipline is the key to controlling impulse buying. If necessary, resort to the self-imposed discipline of the "impulse buying sheet" suggested in figure 4.2.

Establish the discipline that before buying on impulse, you will list the item on the impulse sheet, along with the date and the cost. Furthermore, wait 30 days before purchasing the item and during that time get at least two additional prices.

If you feel you still need the item at the end of the 30 days and the money is available, then buy it. You will eliminate most impulse items by this discipline.

GIFTS

A major budget-buster in most families is overspending on gifts. Tradition dictates a gift for nearly every occasion. Unfortunately, the net result is often a gift someone else doesn't want, purchased with money that was needed for something else.

Many times the cost is increased because the gift is selected at the last moment. If gifts are a part of normal spending, budget for them and buy ahead—reasonably.

To bring the cost of gifts under control, consider doing the following:

1. Keep an event calendar for the year and budget ahead.
2. Determine not to buy any gifts on credit (especially Christmas gifts).
3. Initiate crafts within the family and make some of the needed gifts.
4. Draw family names for selected gifts rather than giving to everyone.

LIST OF DEBTS

TO WHOM OWED	CONTACT PHONE NO.	PAY OFF	PAYMENTS REMAINING	MONTHLY PAYMENT	DUE DATE

IMPULSE LIST					
DATE	IMPULSE ITEM	1	2	3	

Figure 4.2

The Guideline Budget

THE GUIDELINE BUDGET

WHAT IS A GUIDELINE BUDGET?

A guideline budget is family spending divided into percentages to help determine the *proper balance* in each category of the budget, e.g., housing, food, and automobile.

The primary use of the guideline is to *indicate problem areas.* It is *not* an absolute. The percentages are based on a family of four people with incomes ranging from $15,000 to $60,000 per year. Above or below those limits, the percentages may change according to family situations and needs. In the lower income levels, basic family needs will dominate the income distribution. Percentage guidelines are shown in figure 5.1.

PURPOSE OF A GUIDELINE

The guideline is developed to determine a standard against which to compare present spending patterns. It will serve as a basis for determining areas of overspending that are creating the greatest problems. Additionally, it helps to determine where adjustments need to be made. If you are overspending, the percentage guideline can be used as a goal for budgeting. Although the percentages are guides only, and *not* absolute, they do help to establish upper levels of spending.

For instance: A family spending 40 percent or more of their net spendable income on housing will have difficulty balancing their budget. There is little flexibility in most family incomes to absorb excessive spending on housing (or automobiles).

GUIDELINE PERCENTAGES

The *net spendable income* is used to calculate the ideal spending for each budget category. Net spendable income is determined by subtracting your tithe and taxes from your gross income. If taxes are known, then actual amounts can be used. For example, a family of four with an income of $25,000 per year would pay approximately 17.5 percent of gross income in taxes. (For a single person making $12,000 per year, the tax burden will be approximately 19 percent, based on the standard deduction.) In the example shown in figure 5.2 on page 30, net spendable income is $1510 per month. Thus for housing, 38 percent of N.S.I. equals $573 per month. Therefore, no more than $573 per month should be spent for housing, including payment, taxes, utilities, and upkeep.

Note that in some categories absolutes are impossible with variables such as utilities and taxes. You must adjust percentages within ranges under "Housing," "Food," and "Auto." Those three together cannot exceed 65 percent. Example: If 40 percent is used for housing, the percentage for food and auto must be reduced.

The next step? Budget Analysis.

PERCENTAGE GUIDE FOR FAMILY INCOME (Family of Four)					
Gross Income	15,000	25,000	40,000	50,000	60,000
1. Tithe	10%	10%	10%	10%	10%
2. Taxes	8%	17.5%	18%	19%	21%
NET SPENDABLE	12,300	18,125	28,800	35,500	41,400
3. Housing	35%	38%	30%	27%	25%
4. Food	15%	12%	12%	12%	10%
5. Auto	15%	15%	12%	12%	12%
6. Insurance	5%	5%	5%	5%	5%
7. Debts	5%	5%	5%	5%	5%
8. Entertainment/Recreation	5%	5%	7%	7%	7%
9. Clothing	5%	5%	5%	6%	6%
10. Savings	5%	5%	5%	5%	5%
11. Medical/Dental	5%	5%	4%	4%	4%
12. Miscellaneous	5%	5%	7%	8%	8%
13. School/Child Care [1]	10%	8%	6%	5%	5%
14. Investments [2]	—	—	8%	9%	13%
15. Unalloc. Surplus Income [3]	—	—	—	—	—

[1] This category is added as a guide only. If you have this expense, the percentage shown must be deducted from other budget categories.

[2] This category is used for long-term investment planning such as college education or retirement.

[3] This category is used when surplus income is received. This would be kept in the checking account to be used within a few weeks; otherwise, it should be transferred to an allocated category.

Figure 5.1

BUDGET PERCENTAGE GUIDELINES

Salary for guideline =   **$25,000**   **/year**

Gross Income Per Month   **$2083**

1.	Tithe	(10% of Gross)	(2083)	= $	208
2.	Tax	(17.5% of Gross)	(2083)	= $	365

Net Spendable Income   **1510**

3.	Housing	(38% of Net)	(1510)	= $	573
4.	Food	(12% of Net)	(1510)	= $	180
5.	Auto	(15% of Net)	(1510)	= $	225
6.	Insurance	(5% of Net)	(1510)	= $	76
7.	Debts	(5% of Net)	(1510)	= $	76
8.	Entertain. & Rec.	(5% of Net)	(1510)	= $	76
9.	Clothing	(5% of Net)	(1510)	= $	76
10.	Savings	(5% of Net)	(1510)	= $	76
11.	Medical	(5% of Net)	(1510)	= $	76
12.	Miscellaneous	(5% of Net)	(1510)	= $	76
13.	School/ Child Care	(8% of Net) [1]	(_____)	= $	
14.	Investments	(0% of Net) [2]	(_____)	= $	

Total   **(Cannot exceed Net Spendable Income)**   **$ 1510**

15.	Unallocated Surplus Income [3]	(N/A)	= $	

[1] Note: this percentage has *not* been factored into the total percentages shown for net income.

[2] Note: considering the given obligations at this income level, there is no surplus for investing long term.

[3] Note: this category is not part of the budget system but can be used to record and show disbursements of unallocated surplus income. This also provides a good record of income for tax purposes.

Figure 5.2

Budget Analysis

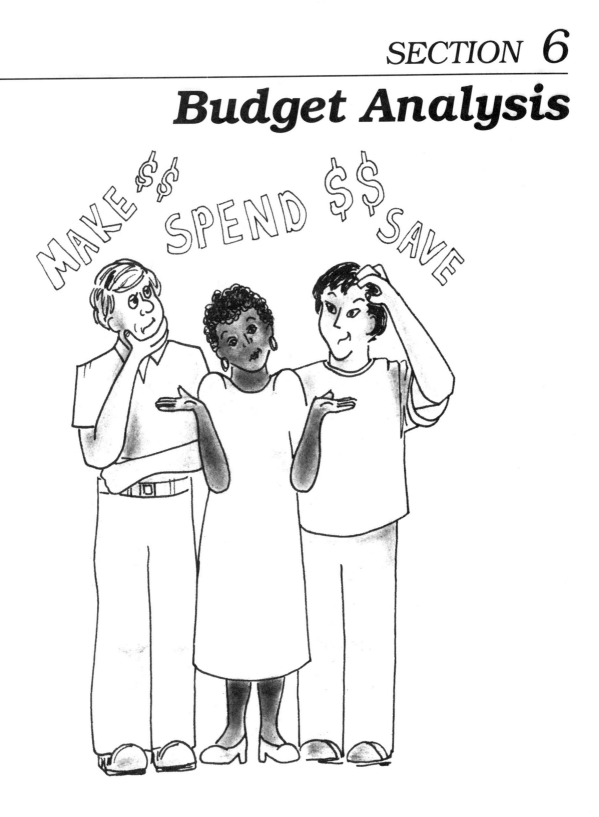

BUDGET ANALYSIS

After determining the present spending level (where you are), and reviewing the guideline percentages (where you should be), the task becomes one of developing a new budget that handles the areas of overspending. Keep in mind that the total expenditures must not exceed the net spendable income. If you have more spendable income than expenses, you need to control spending to maximize your surplus.

The Budget Analysis page (figure 6.1) provides space for summarizing both actual expenses and guideline expenses on one sheet for working convenience. The total amounts of each category from the monthly Income and Expense sheet (figure 2.1) and from the Budget Percentage Guidelines (figure 5.1) should be transferred to the appropriate columns on the Budget Analysis page.

STEP ONE: COMPARE

The *Existing Budget* and *Guideline* columns should be compared. Note the difference, plus or minus, in the *Difference* column. A negative notation indicates a deficit; a positive notation indicates a surplus. The budget shown is the actual spending of a typical family of four.

STEP TWO: ANALYZE

After comparing the *Existing* and *Guideline* columns, decisions must be made about overspending. It may be possible to reduce some areas to compensate for overspending in others. For example, if housing expenditures are more than 38 percent, it may be necessary to sacrifice in such areas as entertainment and recreation, miscellaneous, and automobiles. If debts exceed 5 percent, then the problems are compounded. Ultimately, the decision becomes one of where and how to cut back.

It is not necessary that your new budget fit the guideline budget. It is necessary that your new budget not exceed Net Spendable Income.

It is usually at this point that the husband-wife communication is so important. No one person can make a budget work, because it may involve a family financial sacrifice. Without a willingness to sacrifice and establish discipline, no budget will succeed.

Note the flexibility gained if the family is not in debt. That 5 percent is available for use somewhere else in the budget.

STEP THREE: DECIDE

Once the total picture is reviewed, it is necessary to decide where adjustments must be made and spending reduced. It may be necessary to consider a change in housing, automobiles, insurance, private schools, etc.

The *minimum* objective of any budget should be to meet the family's needs without creating any further debt.

BUDGET ANALYSIS

Per Year __$25,000__   Net Spendable Income Per Month __$1510__

Per Month __$2083__

MONTHLY PAYMENT CATEGORY	EXISTING BUDGET	MONTHLY GUIDELINE BUDGET	DIFFERENCE + OR -	NEW MONTHLY BUDGET
1. Tithe	125	208	+ 83	208
2. Taxes	500	365	– 135	365
NET SPENDABLE INCOME (Per Month)	$ 1458	$ 1510	$ + 52	$ 1510
3. Housing	573	573	0	573
4. Food	230	180	– 50	200
5. Automobile(s)	285	225	– 60	260
6. Insurance	39	76	+ 37	39
7. Debts	90	76	– 14	90
8. Enter. & Recreation	100	76	– 24	76
9. Clothing	50	76	+ 26	70
10. Savings	0	76	+ 76	76
11. Medical	20	76	+ 56	50
12. Miscellaneous	145	76	– 69	76
13. School/Child Care [1]	0	120	+ 120	0
14. Investments	0	N/A	0	0
TOTALS (Items 3–12, 14, 15)	$ 1532	$ 1510	/////	$ 1510
15. Unallocated Surplus Income [2]	0	N/A	0	+ 61

[1] This category not included in totals.

[2] This amount was derived from a garage sale. It is not part of your monthly budget. See page 41.

Figure 6.1

If there are debt problems, then begin by destroying all credit cards and other sources of credit. It may be necessary to negotiate with creditors to pay smaller amounts per month. It's better to establish an amount you can pay than to promise an amount you cannot.

Beware of consolidation loans, refinancing, and more borrowing. They are not the solutions; they are merely "symptom" treatments. The solution comes from discipline, sacrifice, and trusting God to supply needs.

After a new budget has been determined, you are ready to proceed to the allocation and control system.

How the adjustments were made:

1. **Tithe:** The tithe was increased to 10% of gross income.

2. **Taxes:** Taxes were reduced because actual taxes with respect to gross income were less than withholding when all deductions were considered. This was done by increasing the W-4 exemptions by one.

3. **Housing:** No adjustment was made since the housing allocation fit the family's present needs.

4. **Food:** Note 16 percent of Net Spendable Income was being spent. A target amount of $200 was set. Perhaps this can be improved upon with wise shopping.

5. **Auto:** Nearly 20 percent of Net Spendable Income was being spent. Transportation will be adjusted to $260 per month by reducing the insurance coverage.

6. **Insurance:** No change. A close evaluation of insurance needs and types of insurance may be necessary in the future.

7. **Debts:** More than 6% was allocated to existing debts. Credit cards were cancelled. This shows commitment and paves the way for paying off these debts totally in future months.

8. **Enter. & Rec.:** This category was reduced to $76 per month, at least until debts are paid. Caution: Don't cut this out; cut it back.

9. **Clothing:** This category was underbudgeted. The allocation was increased to $70 per month.

10. **Savings:** This was increased to $76. Get in the habit. It's the protection against future debt.

11. **Medical:** This was another underallocation. It was increased to $50 per month.

12. **Miscellaneous:** This category was reduced to $76 per month. If it's not enough, then you will probably have to reduce entertainment and recreation or clothes.

13. **School/Child Care:** No attempt was made to budget for this category. If funds are needed in your budget, the other categories must be adjusted accordingly.

14. **Investments:** Once an adequate emergency fund is established, additional income may be invested for long-term goals.

15. **Unallocated Surplus Income:** Since there is $61 surplus income this month from a garage sale, it will be placed in this category for future use as needed or directed to debt reduction or investments.

SECTION 7

The Control System

ACCOUNTING – ALLOCATION – CONTROL

A budget that is not used is a waste of time and effort. The most common reason a budget is discarded is because it's too complicated.

The system described in this workbook is the simplest, yet most complete possible.

KEEP IT SIMPLE

The Goal — Establish a level of spending for each category such that more money in does not mean more money to spend, and know where you are with respect to that level at all times.

This budget system is analogous to the old "envelope system." In the past, many employers paid earnings in cash. To control spending, families established an effective system by dividing the available money into the various budget categories (housing, food, clothes, etc.), then holding it in individual envelopes.

As a need or payment came due, money was withdrawn from the appropriate envelope and spent.

The system was simple and, when used properly, quite effective for controlling spending. The rule was simple: When an envelope was empty, there was no more spending for that category. Money could be taken from another envelope, but a decision had to be made—immediately.

Since most families today get paid by check, and since holding cash in the home is not always advisable, a different cash allocation system is necessary.

It is important to know how much *should* be spent, how much is being spent and how much is *left* to spend in each budget category. To accomplish this, account control pages have been substituted for envelopes. All the money is deposited into a checking account and account control pages are used to accomplish what the envelopes once accomplished. How much is put into each account (or envelope) from monies received during the month is determined from the Income Allocation sheet.

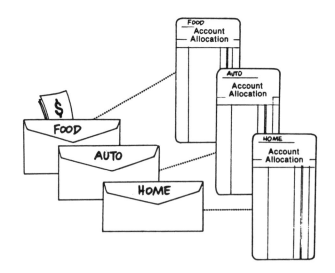

USE OF THE INCOME ALLOCATION PAGE (form 5)

The purpose of the income allocation page is to divide net spendable income among the various budget categories. It is simply a predetermined plan of how each paycheck or income source is going to be spent.

Once you have determined from the budget analysis how much can be spent in each category per month, write it in the *Monthly Allocation* column.

Next, divide the monthly allocation for each category (housing, food, etc.) by pay period.

> EXAMPLE: Family income is received twice each month. Note that the mortgage payment is made on the twenty-ninth of the month so the allocation must be divided in a manner to make sure that adequate funds are available at the time the payment is due. Utility and maintenance payments would have to be made from another pay period.

	ALLOCATION	PAY PERIOD	
HOUSING	$573	$423	$150
FOOD	$200	$100	$100
AUTO	$260	$160	$100
INSURANCE	$ 39	$ 14	$ 25

It is not mandatory that checks be divided evenly. The important thing is that when a payment is due that the money be available. Therefore, some reserve funds from middle-of-the-month pay periods must be held to meet obligations that come due at the first of the month. Failure to do this is a common source of budget problems.

USE OF THE INDIVIDUAL ACCOUNT PAGES (form 7)
(Refer to figure 7.1)

A separate account page is used for each budget category (housing, food, auto, etc.) just as each had its own envelope under the cash system.

At the top of the page, the proper account title is entered (housing, food, etc.) together with the monthly allocation. Each account sheet has two blanks ($_____). These are used to write in your allocation for a twice monthly pay period. If you are paid more frequently, just add more blanks ($_____). This will help you to remember how much to write in each pay period.

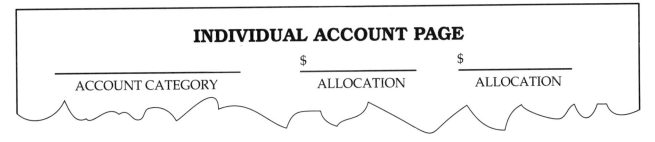

INDIVIDUAL ACCOUNT PAGE

| ACCOUNT CATEGORY | $ ALLOCATION | $ ALLOCATION |

The purpose of the account sheet is to document ALL transactions for the month. The pay period allowance or allocation is shown as a deposit, and each time money is spent, it is shown as a withdrawal.

If funds are left at the end of the month, the account page is zeroed by transferrring the money to the savings account. If an account runs short, then it may be necessary to transfer money from savings to the appropriate account. When an account is out of money, a decision must be made concerning how it is going to be treated.

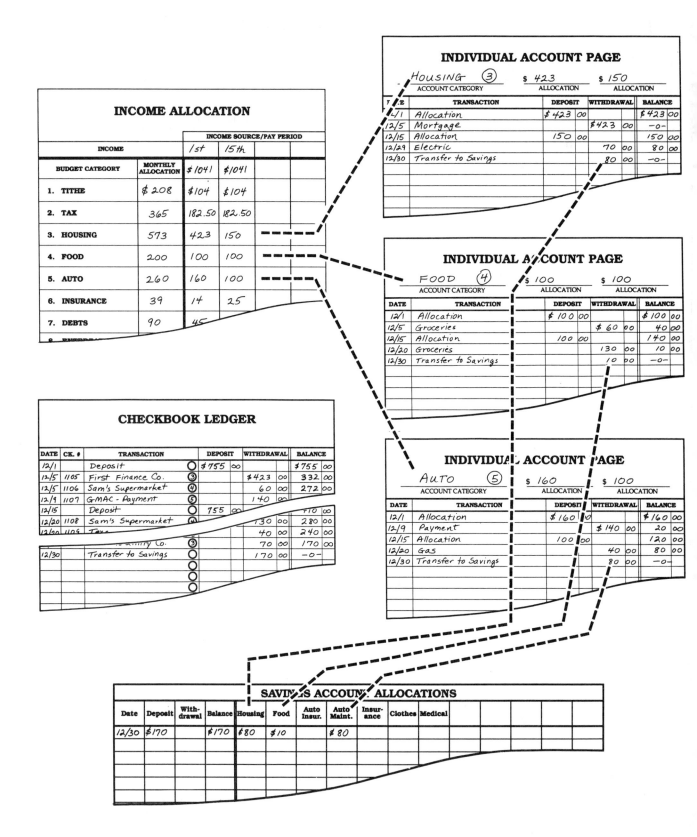

INCOME ALLOCATION

		INCOME SOURCE/PAY PERIOD		
INCOME		1st	15th	
BUDGET CATEGORY	MONTHLY ALLOCATION	$1041	$1041	
1. TITHE	$208	$104	$104	
2. TAX	365	182.50	182.50	
3. HOUSING	573	423	150	
4. FOOD	200	100	100	
5. AUTO	260	160	100	
6. INSURANCE	39	14	25	
7. DEBTS	90	45		

INDIVIDUAL ACCOUNT PAGE

HOUSING ③ $423 $150
ACCOUNT CATEGORY   ALLOCATION   ALLOCATION

DATE	TRANSACTION	DEPOSIT	WITHDRAWAL	BALANCE
12/1	Allocation	$423 00		$423 00
12/5	Mortgage		$423 00	-0-
12/15	Allocation	150 00		150 00
12/29	Electric		70 00	80 00
12/30	Transfer to Savings		80 00	-0-

INDIVIDUAL ACCOUNT PAGE

FOOD ④ $100 $100
ACCOUNT CATEGORY   ALLOCATION   ALLOCATION

DATE	TRANSACTION	DEPOSIT	WITHDRAWAL	BALANCE
12/1	Allocation	$100 00		$100 00
12/5	Groceries		$60 00	40 00
12/15	Allocation	100 00		140 00
12/20	Groceries		130 00	10 00
12/30	Transfer to Savings		10 00	-0-

CHECKBOOK LEDGER

DATE	CK. #	TRANSACTION		DEPOSIT	WITHDRAWAL	BALANCE
12/1		Deposit	○	$755 00		$755 00
12/5	1105	First Finance Co.	③		$423 00	332 00
12/5	1106	Sam's Supermarket	④		60 00	272 00
12/9	1107	GMAC - Payment	⑤		140 00	
12/15		Deposit	○	755 00		710 00
12/20	1108	Sam's Supermarket	④		130 00	280 00
12/20	1109	Tax			40 00	240 00
		...nity Co.	③		70 00	170 00
12/30		Transfer to Savings	○		170 00	-0-

INDIVIDUAL ACCOUNT PAGE

AUTO ⑤ $160 $100
ACCOUNT CATEGORY   ALLOCATION   ALLOCATION

DATE	TRANSACTION	DEPOSIT	WITHDRAWAL	BALANCE
12/1	Allocation	$160 00		$160 00
12/9	Payment		$140 00	20 00
12/15	Allocation	100 00		120 00
12/20	Gas		40 00	80 00
12/30	Transfer to Savings		80 00	-0-

SAVINGS ACCOUNT ALLOCATIONS

Date	Deposit	With-drawal	Balance	Housing	Food	Auto Insur.	Auto Maint.	Insur-ance	Clothes	Medical			
12/30	$170		$170	$80	$10		$80						

Figure 7.1

HOW TO USE THE BUDGET SYSTEM

A good budget system should be kept as simple as possible while still accomplishing its goal: *To tell you if you spend more that you allocated each month.* Remember that this system is analogous to using envelopes. If a specific amount of money is placed in the envelopes each month, you will know at a glance whether or not your budget balances. Obviously with some non-monthly expenses to be budgeted the ledger system has to be a little more complicated, but don't *over*complicate it.

To help you better understand how to use the budget system, we will take one category (housing) through a typical month's transactions.

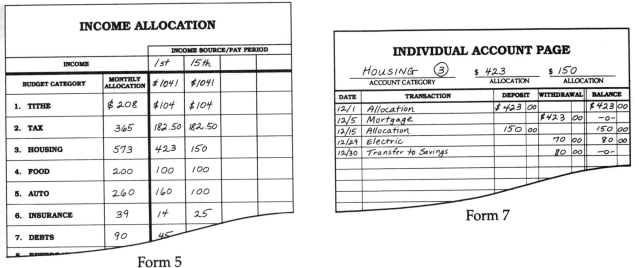

Form 5

Form 7

Figure 7.2

Figure 7.2 shows a typical family budget in which the gross income of $2083 per month is received in two pay periods of $1041 each.

PAY ALLOCATION — The two checks have been divided as evenly as possible among the necessary categories. For example, the tithe is paid each pay period (remember, it is based on gross income). The housing allocation of $573 is divided, $423 in the first pay period, $150 in the second.

HOUSING ALLOCATION — On the first pay period, a deposit of $423 is noted on the account page. On the fifth, the mortgage is paid and noted as a withdrawal, leaving a balance of $0.

Each transaction is noted similarly until, at the end of the month, a balance of $80 is left. This balance is then transferred to savings, as are month-end balances from the other account pages (food, savings, etc.). Hence, each account starts at zero the next month.

Many people prefer to leave the surplus funds from each category in their checking account rather than transfer them to a savings account. This is fine provided that you can discipline yourself not to spend the money just because it's easily accessible. Often the total cash reserves in checking are enough to qualify for free checking privileges, which more than offset any loss of interest in a savings account.

NOTE: In many cases, the housing account may have to carry a surplus forward to make the mortgage payment if it comes due on the first.

USE OF THE CHECKBOOK LEDGER

To simplify your bookkeeping, I recommend using one of the Account Allocation Sheets (form 7) as a checkbook ledger. If you also use a checkbook that gives you a carbon copy of each check written, it will reduce the number of steps in the bookkeeping process.

Note that the checkbook ledger (form 7a) is just a slightly modified form 7. Each deposit and withdrawal is recorded, and the outstanding balance is shown. At the end of each month the ledger is balanced against the bank statement. Also, the total balance in the ledger is then compared to the balance on the budget account sheets.

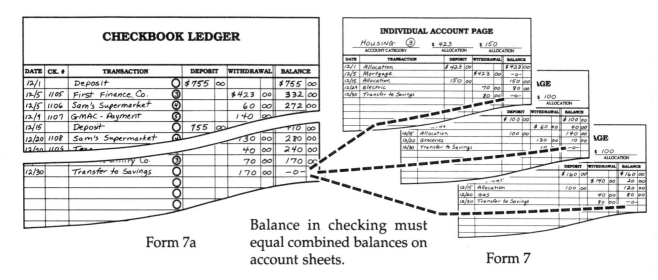

Form 7a

Balance in checking must equal combined balances on account sheets.

Form 7

If there are additional deposits or withdrawals from the bank statement recorded in the checkbook ledger, these must also be posted in the appropriate budget account sheets. For example, a service charge from the bank would be posted as an expense in the checkbook ledger and as a miscellaneous expense in category 12 of the budget.

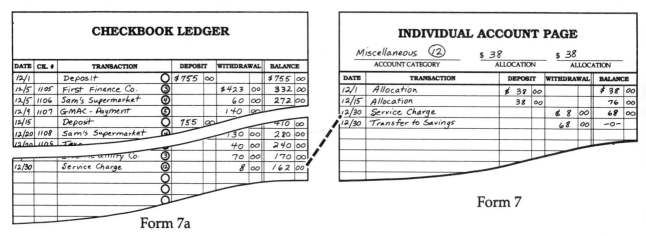

Form 7a

Form 7

Note that the circle (○) on form 7a is used to indicate the category to which the check has been allocated in the budget. This is filled in *only* after the check has been recorded in the proper budget category.

CHECKING ACCOUNT NOTATION

The common practice with many budgeters is to write the checks, record (post) the checks in the home ledger (figure 7.3), and then record the transactions in the budget account sheets at a later time. To insure that all checks are recorded in the account sheets, a notation of the category number should be made for each entry in the checkbook ledger in the appropriate block.

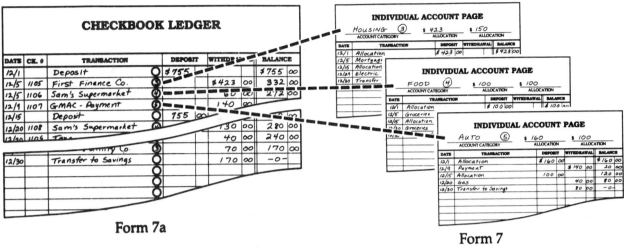

Form 7a

Form 7

Figure 7.3

Keep in mind that the goal of the system is to establish a level of spending for each category and to know where you are with respect to that level.

The account pages ("envelopes") keep track of money in the checking account. The savings allocation page keeps track of money in the savings account. However, you may want to use a savings account page (or envelope) within the checking account to minimize transfers to and from the savings account.

Remember—the plan is to know what each dollar in the checking account is for and what each dollar in the savings account is for. When you spend money, you need to know which money is spent (clothes money, food money, gas money, etc.).

USE OF CATEGORY 15 — SURPLUS INCOME

I have found in using the budget system myself that sometimes I had extra money available above that which I had budgeted. I could have simply tranferred it to my savings category, and often did so if the money was to be used several months later. But if the money was going to be used within a few weeks, I wanted to leave it in the checking account. Since I didn't want it allocated to any of the regular monthly categories, I created a fifteenth category just to hold these surplus funds. This allowed me to keep each of the other categories constant each month. You may find this system helpful if you periodically have extra income that is unallocated. It also serves as a good record of income for tax purposes.

DISCIPLINE

In order to provide the necessary control, you must discipline yourself to spend money based on the bottom line of the applicable envelope and not based on the bottom line of the checkbook.

POTENTIAL PROBLEM AREAS

CASH WITHDRAWALS — Many times miscellaneous expenditures for car expenses, gas, etc. are made with personal cash. In establishing a budget, it is important to develop some rules for self-discipline.

1. Separate personal cash into categories identical to the account pages. Use envelopes if necessary, but avoid spending gas money for lunches and grocery money for entertainment.

2. When all the money has been spent from a category (entertainment, lunches, etc.) *stop spending.*

3. Don't write checks for amounts in excess of actual purchases to get cash. Write another check and note it as "cash, personal."

CATEGORY MIXING — Don't try to make the record-keeping more complicated than necessary. This system should require no more than thirty minutes per week to maintain. If you choose to develop more detailed breakdowns of expenses and savings, wait until the budget has been in use at least six months.

AUTOMATIC OVERDRAFTS

Many banks offer an automatic overdraft protection service. Thus if you write a check in excess of what you have in your account, the bank will still honor it. On the surface this looks like a helpful service. However, it has been my experience that the overdraft protection tends to create a complacent attitude about balancing the account and encourages overdrafting. Since these charges are accrued to a credit account, you will end up paying interest on your overdrafts. I recommend that these services be avoided until the budgeting routine is well established. Hopefully by then they will be unnecessary.

BUDGETING ON A VARIABLE INCOME

One of the most difficult problems in budgeting is how to allocate monthly spending when your income fluctuates, as it often does on commission sales. The normal tendency is to spend the money as it comes in. This works great during the high income months but usually causes havoc during the lower income months.

Two suggestions will help anyone living on a fluctuating income: First, always separate any business-related expenses such as car maintenance, meals, living accommodations, etc., from your normal household expenses. I recommend a separate checking account for business expenses and separate credit cards, if needed.

Second, you need to estimate what your (low) average income for one year will be and generate your monthly budget based on the "average" income per month. As the funds come in they need to be deposited in a special savings account and a salary drawn from the account. The effect is to ration the income over the year in relatively equal amounts that can be budgeted.

Remember that if you are self-employed, you will need to budget for payroll taxes on a quarterly basis. Failure to do this will result in a rather unpleasant visit with representatives of the Internal Revenue Service.

If you are beginning your budget during one of the lower income months, you may have to delay funding some of the variable expenses such as clothing, vacations, dental, etc. These can be funded later when the income allows.

WHAT IF YOU ARE PAID EVERY TWO WEEKS?

If you happen to be one of those families paid every two weeks rather than twice monthly, you will have two extra paychecks a year. I recommend using these paychecks to fund some of the non-monthly expenses such as car repair, vacation, clothing, etc. The same would be true of tax refunds, bonuses, and gifts.

SECTION *8*

Begin Now

MONTHLY INCOME & EXPENSES

GROSS INCOME PER MONTH 1100.00

    Salary   _____

    Interest   _____

    Dividends   _____

    Other   _____

LESS:

  1. **Tithe**   200.00

  2. **Tax** (Est. - Incl. Fed., State, FICA)   _____

  NET SPENDABLE INCOME _____

  3. **Housing**   85.00

    Mortgage (rent)   0

    Insurance   0

    Taxes   0

    Electricity   0

    Gas   0

    Water   0

    Sanitation   0

    Telephone   55.00

    Maintenance

    Other *TV*   45.00

  4. **Food**   65

  5. **Automobile(s)**   150

    Payments   0

    Gas & Oil   40

    Insurance   61.00

    License/Taxes   20.00

    Maint./Repair/Replace   20

  6. **Insurance**   0

    Life   0

    Medical   0

    Other   0

  7. **Debts**   0

    Credit Card   0

    Loans & Notes   0

    Other   0

  8. **Enter. & Recreation**   _____

    Eating Out   20

    Baby Sitters   0

    Activities/Trips

    Vacation

    Other *BB cards*   150

  9. **Clothing**   10

 10. **Savings**   20

 11. **Medical Expenses**   10

    Doctor   0

    Dentist   0

    Drugs   0

    Other   0

 12. **Miscellaneous**   90

    Toiletry, cosmetics   5

    Beauty, barber   10

    Laundry, cleaning   2

    Allowances, lunches   0

    Subscriptions   13

    Gifts (incl. Christmas)   60

    Cash

    Other

 13. **School/Child Care**   0

    Tuition   0

    Materials   0

    Transportation   0

    Day Care   0

 14. **Investments**   _____

 TOTAL EXPENSES _____

INCOME VS. EXPENSES

    Net Spendable Income   _____

    Less Expenses   _____

 15. **Unallocated Surplus Income** [1]   _____

[1] This category is used when surplus income is received. This would be kept in the checking account to be used within a few weeks; otherwise, it should be transferred to an allocated category. See page 41 for further information.

FORM 1

MONTHLY INCOME & EXPENSES

GROSS INCOME PER MONTH _____

   Salary _____

   Interest _____

   Dividends _____

   Other _____

LESS:

1. **Tithe** _____

2. **Tax** (Est. - Incl. Fed., State, FICA) _____

NET SPENDABLE INCOME _____

3. **Housing** _____

   Mortgage (rent) _____

   Insurance _____

   Taxes _____

   Electricity _____

   Gas _____

   Water _____

   Sanitation _____

   Telephone _____

   Maintenance _____

   Other _____

4. **Food** _____

5. **Automobile(s)** _____

   Payments _____

   Gas & Oil _____

   Insurance _____

   License/Taxes _____

   Maint./Repair/Replace _____

6. **Insurance** _____

   Life _____

   Medical _____

   Other _____

7. **Debts** _____

   Credit Card _____

   Loans & Notes _____

   Other _____

8. **Enter. & Recreation** _____

   Eating Out _____

   Baby Sitters _____

   Activities/Trips _____

   Vacation _____

   Other _____

9. **Clothing** _____

10. **Savings** _____

11. **Medical Expenses** _____

   Doctor _____

   Dentist _____

   Drugs _____

   Other _____

12. **Miscellaneous** _____

   Toiletry, cosmetics _____

   Beauty, barber _____

   Laundry, cleaning _____

   Allowances, lunches _____

   Subscriptions _____

   Gifts (incl. Christmas) _____

   Cash _____

   Other _____

13. **School/Child Care** _____

   Tuition _____

   Materials _____

   Transportation _____

   Day Care _____

14. **Investments** _____

TOTAL EXPENSES _____

INCOME VS. EXPENSES

   Net Spendable Income _____

   Less Expenses _____

15. **Unallocated Surplus Income** [1] _____

[1] This category is used when surplus income is received. This would be kept in the checking account to be used within a few weeks; otherwise, it should be transferred to an allocated category. See page 41 for further information.

FORM 1

MONTHLY INCOME & EXPENSES

GROSS INCOME PER MONTH _____

    Salary _____

    Interest _____

    Dividends _____

    Other _____

LESS:

  1. **Tithe** _____

  2. **Tax** (Est. - Incl. Fed., State, FICA) _____

    NET SPENDABLE INCOME _____

  3. **Housing** _____

    Mortgage (rent) _____

    Insurance _____

    Taxes _____

    Electricity _____

    Gas _____

    Water _____

    Sanitation _____

    Telephone _____

    Maintenance _____

    Other _____

  4. **Food** _____

  5. **Automobile(s)** _____

    Payments _____

    Gas & Oil _____

    Insurance _____

    License/Taxes _____

    Maint./Repair/Replace _____

  6. **Insurance** _____

    Life _____

    Medical _____

    Other _____

  7. **Debts** _____

    Credit Card _____

    Loans & Notes _____

    Other _____

  8. **Enter. & Recreation** _____

    Eating Out _____

    Baby Sitters _____

    Activities/Trips _____

    Vacation _____

    Other _____

  9. **Clothing** _____

  10. **Savings** _____

  11. **Medical Expenses** _____

    Doctor _____

    Dentist _____

    Drugs _____

    Other _____

  12. **Miscellaneous** _____

    Toiletry, cosmetics _____

    Beauty, barber _____

    Laundry, cleaning _____

    Allowances, lunches _____

    Subscriptions _____

    Gifts (incl. Christmas) _____

    Cash _____

    Other _____

  13. **School/Child Care** _____

    Tuition _____

    Materials _____

    Transportation _____

    Day Care _____

  14. **Investments** _____

    TOTAL EXPENSES _____

INCOME VS. EXPENSES

    Net Spendable Income _____

    Less Expenses _____

  15. **Unallocated Surplus Income** [1] _____

[1] This category is used when surplus income is received. This would be kept in the checking account to be used within a few weeks; otherwise, it should be transferred to an allocated category. See page 41 for further information.

FORM 1

MONTHLY INCOME & EXPENSES

GROSS INCOME PER MONTH _____

   Salary _____

   Interest _____

   Dividends _____

   Other _____

LESS:

  1. Tithe _____

  2. Tax (Est. - Incl. Fed., State, FICA) _____

NET SPENDABLE INCOME _____

  3. Housing _____

   Mortgage (rent) _____

   Insurance _____

   Taxes _____

   Electricity _____

   Gas _____

   Water _____

   Sanitation _____

   Telephone _____

   Maintenance _____

   Other _____

  4. Food _____

  5. Automobile(s) _____

   Payments _____

   Gas & Oil _____

   Insurance _____

   License/Taxes _____

   Maint./Repair/Replace _____

  6. Insurance _____

   Life _____

   Medical _____

   Other _____

  7. Debts _____

   Credit Card _____

   Loans & Notes _____

   Other _____

  8. Enter. & Recreation _____

   Eating Out _____

   Baby Sitters _____

   Activities/Trips _____

   Vacation _____

   Other _____

  9. Clothing _____

  10. Savings _____

  11. Medical Expenses _____

   Doctor _____

   Dentist _____

   Drugs _____

   Other _____

  12. Miscellaneous _____

   Toiletry, cosmetics _____

   Beauty, barber _____

   Laundry, cleaning _____

   Allowances, lunches _____

   Subscriptions _____

   Gifts (incl. Christmas) _____

   Cash _____

   Other _____

  13. School/Child Care _____

   Tuition _____

   Materials _____

   Transportation _____

   Day Care _____

  14. Investments _____

TOTAL EXPENSES _____

INCOME VS. EXPENSES

  Net Spendable Income _____

  Less Expenses _____

  15. Unallocated Surplus Income [1] _____

[1] This category is used when surplus income is received. This would be kept in the checking account to be used within a few weeks; otherwise, it should be transferred to an allocated category. See page 41 for further information.

FORM 1

VARIABLE EXPENSE PLANNING

Plan for those expenses that are not paid on a regular monthly basis by estimating the yearly cost and determining the monthly amount needed to be set aside for that expense. A helpful formula is to allow the previous year's expense and add 5 percent.

		Estimated Cost		Per Month
1.	VACATION	$_____	÷ 12 =	$_____
2.	DENTIST	$_____	÷ 12 =	$_____
3.	DOCTOR	$_____	÷ 12 =	$_____
4.	AUTOMOBILE	$_____	÷ 12 =	$_____
5.	ANNUAL INSURANCE	$_____	÷ 12 =	$_____
	(Life)	($_____	÷ 12 =	$_____)
	(Health)	($_____	÷ 12 =	$_____)
	(Auto)	($_____	÷ 12 =	$_____)
	(Home)	($_____	÷ 12 =	$_____)
6.	CLOTHING	$_____	÷ 12 =	$_____
7.	INVESTMENTS	$_____	÷ 12 =	$_____
8.	OTHER	$_____	÷ 12 =	$_____
		$_____	÷ 12 =	$_____

FORM 2

VARIABLE EXPENSE PLANNING

Plan for those expenses that are not paid on a regular monthly basis by estimating the yearly cost and determining the monthly amount needed to be set aside for that expense. A helpful formula is to allow the previous year's expense and add 5 percent.

		Estimated Cost	Per Month
1.	VACATION	$_____ ÷ 12 =	$_____
2.	DENTIST	$_____ ÷ 12 =	$_____
3.	DOCTOR	$_____ ÷ 12 =	$_____
4.	AUTOMOBILE	$_____ ÷ 12 =	$_____
5.	ANNUAL INSURANCE	$_____ ÷ 12 =	$_____
	(Life)	($_____ ÷ 12 =	$_____)
	(Health)	($_____ ÷ 12 =	$_____)
	(Auto)	($_____ ÷ 12 =	$_____)
	(Home)	($_____ ÷ 12 =	$_____)
6.	CLOTHING	$_____ ÷ 12 =	$_____
7.	INVESTMENTS	$_____ ÷ 12 =	$_____
8.	OTHER	$_____ ÷ 12 =	$_____
		$_____ ÷ 12 =	$_____

FORM 2

VARIABLE EXPENSE PLANNING

Plan for those expenses that are not paid on a regular monthly basis by estimating the yearly cost and determining the monthly amount needed to be set aside for that expense. A helpful formula is to allow the previous year's expense and add 5 percent.

	Estimated Cost	Per Month
1. VACATION	$_____ ÷ 12 =	$_____
2. DENTIST	$_____ ÷ 12 =	$_____
3. DOCTOR	$_____ ÷ 12 =	$_____
4. AUTOMOBILE	$_____ ÷ 12 =	$_____
5. ANNUAL INSURANCE	$_____ ÷ 12 =	$_____
(Life)	($_____ ÷ 12 =	$_____)
(Health)	($_____ ÷ 12 =	$_____)
(Auto)	($_____ ÷ 12 =	$_____)
(Home)	($_____ ÷ 12 =	$_____)
6. CLOTHING	$_____ ÷ 12 =	$_____
7. INVESTMENTS	$_____ ÷ 12 =	$_____
8. OTHER	$_____ ÷ 12 =	$_____
	$_____ ÷ 12 =	$_____

FORM 2

VARIABLE EXPENSE PLANNING

Plan for those expenses that are not paid on a regular monthly basis by estimating the yearly cost and determining the monthly amount needed to be set aside for that expense. A helpful formula is to allow the previous year's expense and add 5 percent.

		Estimated Cost	Per Month
1.	VACATION	$ _____ ÷ 12 = $ _____
2.	DENTIST	$ _____ ÷ 12 = $ _____
3.	DOCTOR	$ _____ ÷ 12 = $ _____
4.	AUTOMOBILE	$ _____ ÷ 12 = $ _____
5.	ANNUAL INSURANCE	$ _____ ÷ 12 = $ _____
	(Life)	($ _____ ÷ 12 = $ _____)
	(Health)	($ _____ ÷ 12 = $ _____)
	(Auto)	($ _____ ÷ 12 = $ _____)
	(Home)	($ _____ ÷ 12 = $ _____)
6.	CLOTHING	$ _____ ÷ 12 = $ _____
7.	INVESTMENTS	$ _____ ÷ 12 = $ _____
8.	OTHER	$ _____ ÷ 12 = $ _____
		$ _____ ÷ 12 = $ _____

FORM 2

BUDGET PERCENTAGE GUIDELINES

Salary for guideline = _____ /year [1]

Gross Income Per Month _____

   1. **Tithe**   (___ % of Gross)   (_____)   = $ _____

   2. **Tax**   (___ % of Gross)   (_____)   = $ _____

Net Spendable Income   _____

   3. **Housing**   (___ % of Net)   (_____)   = $ _____

   4. **Food**   (___ % of Net)   (_____)   = $ _____

   5. **Auto**   (___ % of Net)   (_____)   = $ _____

   6. **Insurance**   (___ % of Net)   (_____)   = $ _____

   7. **Debts**   (___ % of Net)   (_____)   = $ _____

   8. **Entertain. & Rec.**   (___ % of Net)   (_____)   = $ _____

   9. **Clothing**   (___ % of Net)   (_____)   = $ _____

  10. **Savings**   (___ % of Net)   (_____)   = $ _____

  11. **Medical**   (___ % of Net)   (_____)   = $ _____

  12. **Miscellaneous**   (___ % of Net)   (_____)   = $ _____

  13. **School/ Child Care**   (___ % of Net)   (_____)   = $ _____

  14. **Investments**   (___ % of Net)   (_____)   = $ _____

Total   **(Cannot exceed Net Spendable Income)** $ _____

  15. **Unallocated Surplus Income**   (__N/A__)   = $ _____

[1] Refer to page 29 for percentage guidelines.

FORM 3

BUDGET PERCENTAGE GUIDELINES

Salary for guideline = _____ /year [1]

Gross Income Per Month _____

   1. Tithe   (__ % of Gross)   (_____) = $ _____

   2. Tax   (__ % of Gross)   (_____) = $ _____

Net Spendable Income   _____

   3. Housing   (__ % of Net)   (_____) = $ _____

   4. Food   (__ % of Net)   (_____) = $ _____

   5. Auto   (__ % of Net)   (_____) = $ _____

   6. Insurance   (__ % of Net)   (_____) = $ _____

   7. Debts   (__ % of Net)   (_____) = $ _____

   8. Entertain. (__ % of Net)   (_____) = $ _____
       & Rec.

   9. Clothing   (__ % of Net)   (_____) = $ _____

  10. Savings   (__ % of Net)   (_____) = $ _____

  11. Medical   (__ % of Net)   (_____) = $ _____

  12. Miscellaneous (__ % of Net)   (_____) = $ _____

  13. School/   (__ % of Net)   (_____) = $ _____
       Child Care

  14. Investments (__ % of Net)   (_____) = $ _____

Total (Cannot exceed Net Spendable Income) $ _____

  15. Unallocated Surplus Income   (__N/A__) = $ _____

Refer to page 29 for percentage guidelines.

FORM 3

BUDGET PERCENTAGE GUIDELINES

Salary for guideline = _____/year [1]

Gross Income Per Month _____

  1. **Tithe** (___ % of Gross) (_____) = $ _____

  2. **Tax** (___ % of Gross) (_____) = $ _____

Net Spendable Income _____

  3. **Housing** (___ % of Net) (_____) = $ _____

  4. **Food** (___ % of Net) (_____) = $ _____

  5. **Auto** (___ % of Net) (_____) = $ _____

  6. **Insurance** (___ % of Net) (_____) = $ _____

  7. **Debts** (___ % of Net) (_____) = $ _____

  8. **Entertain. & Rec.** (___ % of Net) (_____) = $ _____

  9. **Clothing** (___ % of Net) (_____) = $ _____

  10. **Savings** (___ % of Net) (_____) = $ _____

  11. **Medical** (___ % of Net) (_____) = $ _____

  12. **Miscellaneous** (___ % of Net) (_____) = $ _____

  13. **School/ Child Care** (___ % of Net) (_____) = $ _____

  14. **Investments** (___ % of Net) (_____) = $ _____

Total **(Cannot exceed Net Spendable Income)** $ _____

  15. **Unallocated Surplus Income** (__N/A__) = $ _____

[1] Refer to page 29 for percentage guidelines.

FORM 3

BUDGET PERCENTAGE GUIDELINES

Salary for guideline = _____ /year [1]

Gross Income Per Month _____

   1. Tithe   (__ % of Gross) (_____)   = $ _____

   2. Tax   (__ % of Gross) (_____)   = $ _____

Net Spendable Income   _____

   3. Housing   (__ % of Net)   (_____)   = $ _____

   4. Food   (__ % of Net)   (_____)   = $ _____

   5. Auto   (__ % of Net)   (_____)   = $ _____

   6. Insurance (__ % of Net)   (_____)   = $ _____

   7. Debts   (__ % of Net)   (_____)   = $ _____

   8. Entertain. (__ % of Net)   (_____)   = $ _____
        & Rec.

   9. Clothing   (__ % of Net)   (_____)   = $ _____

 10. Savings   (__ % of Net)   (_____)   = $ _____

 11. Medical   (__ % of Net)   (_____)   = $ _____

 12. Miscellaneous (__ % of Net)   (_____)   = $ _____

 13. School/   (__ % of Net)   (_____)   = $ _____
        Child Care

 14. Investments (__ % of Net)   (_____)   = $ _____

Total (Cannot exceed Net Spendable Income) $ _____

 15. Unallocated Surplus Income   (__N/A__)   = $ _____

[1] Refer to page 29 for percentage guidelines.

BUDGET ANALYSIS

Per Year _____ Net Spendable Income Per Month _____

Per Month _____

MONTHLY PAYMENT CATEGORY	EXISTING BUDGET	MONTHLY GUIDELINE BUDGET	DIFFERENCE + OR -	NEW MONTHLY BUDGET
1. Tithe				
2. Taxes				
NET SPENDABLE INCOME (Per Month)	$	$	$	$
3. Housing				
4. Food				
5. Automobile(s)				
6. Insurance				
7. Debts				
8. Enter. & Recreation				
9. Clothing				
10. Savings				
11. Medical				
12. Miscellaneous				
13. School/Child Care				
14. Investments				
TOTALS (Items 3–14)	$	$	////////	$
15. Unallocated Surplus Income				

FORM 4

BUDGET ANALYSIS

Per Year _____ Net Spendable Income Per Month _____

Per Month _____

MONTHLY PAYMENT CATEGORY	EXISTING BUDGET	MONTHLY GUIDELINE BUDGET	DIFFERENCE + OR -	NEW MONTHLY BUDGET
1. Tithe				
2. Taxes				
NET SPENDABLE INCOME (Per Month)	$_____	$_____	$_____	$_____
3. Housing				
4. Food				
5. Automobile(s)				
6. Insurance				
7. Debts				
8. Enter. & Recreation				
9. Clothing				
10. Savings				
11. Medical				
12. Miscellaneous				
13. School/Child Care				
14. Investments				
TOTALS (Items 3–14)	$_____	$_____	/////////	$_____
15. Unallocated Surplus Income				

FORM 4

BUDGET ANALYSIS

Per Year _____ Net Spendable Income Per Month _____

Per Month _____

MONTHLY PAYMENT CATEGORY	EXISTING BUDGET	MONTHLY GUIDELINE BUDGET	DIFFERENCE + OR -	NEW MONTHLY BUDGET
1. Tithe				
2. Taxes				
NET SPENDABLE INCOME (Per Month)	$_____	$_____	$_____	$_____
3. Housing				
4. Food				
5. Automobile(s)				
6. Insurance				
7. Debts				
8. Enter. & Recreation				
9. Clothing				
10. Savings				
11. Medical				
12. Miscellaneous				
13. School/Child Care				
14. Investments				
TOTALS (Items 3–14)	$_____	$_____	/////////	$_____
15. Unallocated Surplus Income				

BUDGET ANALYSIS

Per Year _____ Net Spendable Income Per Month _____

Per Month _____

MONTHLY PAYMENT CATEGORY	EXISTING BUDGET	MONTHLY GUIDELINE BUDGET	DIFFERENCE + OR -	NEW MONTHLY BUDGET
1. Tithe				
2. Taxes				
NET SPENDABLE INCOME (Per Month)	$_____	$_____	$_____	$_____
3. Housing				
4. Food				
5. Automobile(s)				
6. Insurance				
7. Debts				
8. Enter. & Recreation				
9. Clothing				
10. Savings				
11. Medical				
12. Miscellaneous				
13. School/Child Care				
14. Investments				
TOTALS (Items 3–14)	$_____	$_____	/////////	$_____
15. Unallocated Surplus Income				

FORM 4

INCOME ALLOCATION

INCOME		INCOME SOURCE/PAY PERIOD			
BUDGET CATEGORY	MONTHLY ALLOCATION				
1. TITHE					
2. TAX					
3. HOUSING					
4. FOOD					
5. AUTO					
6. INSURANCE					
7. DEBTS					
8. ENTERTAINMENT & RECREATION					
9. CLOTHING					
10. SAVINGS					
11. MEDICAL/DENTAL					
12. MISCELLANEOUS					
13. SCHOOL/ CHILD CARE					
14. INVESTMENTS					
15. UNALLOCATED SURPLUS INCOME					

FORM 5

INCOME ALLOCATION

INCOME		INCOME SOURCE/PAY PERIOD			
BUDGET CATEGORY	MONTHLY ALLOCATION				
1. TITHE					
2. TAX					
3. HOUSING					
4. FOOD					
5. AUTO					
6. INSURANCE					
7. DEBTS					
8. ENTERTAINMENT & RECREATION					
9. CLOTHING					
10. SAVINGS					
11. MEDICAL/DENTAL					
12. MISCELLANEOUS					
13. SCHOOL/ CHILD CARE					
14. INVESTMENTS					
15. UNALLOCATED SURPLUS INCOME					

INCOME ALLOCATION

INCOME		INCOME SOURCE/PAY PERIOD			
BUDGET CATEGORY	MONTHLY ALLOCATION				
1. TITHE					
2. TAX					
3. HOUSING					
4. FOOD					
5. AUTO					
6. INSURANCE					
7. DEBTS					
8. ENTERTAINMENT & RECREATION					
9. CLOTHING					
10. SAVINGS					
11. MEDICAL/DENTAL					
12. MISCELLANEOUS					
13. SCHOOL/ CHILD CARE					
14. INVESTMENTS					
15. UNALLOCATED SURPLUS INCOME					

FORM 5

INCOME ALLOCATION

INCOME		INCOME SOURCE/PAY PERIOD			
BUDGET CATEGORY	MONTHLY ALLOCATION				
1. TITHE					
2. TAX					
3. HOUSING					
4. FOOD					
5. AUTO					
6. INSURANCE					
7. DEBTS					
8. ENTERTAINMENT & RECREATION					
9. CLOTHING					
10. SAVINGS					
11. MEDICAL/DENTAL					
12. MISCELLANEOUS					
13. SCHOOL/ CHILD CARE					
14. INVESTMENTS					
15. UNALLOCATED SURPLUS INCOME					

SAVINGS ACCOUNT ALLOCATIONS

Date	Deposit	With-drawal	Balance	Housing	Food	Auto Insur.	Auto Maint.	Insur-ance	Clothes	Medical						

FORM 6

SAVINGS ACCOUNT ALLOCATIONS

Date	Deposit	With-drawal	Balance	Housing	Food	Auto Insur.	Auto Maint.	Insur-ance	Clothes	Medical

FORM 6

SAVINGS ACCOUNT ALLOCATIONS

Date	Deposit	With-drawal	Balance	Housing	Food	Auto Insur.	Auto Maint.	Insur-ance	Clothes	Medical					

FORM 6

SAVINGS ACCOUNT ALLOCATIONS

Date	Deposit	With-drawal	Balance	Housing	Food	Auto Insur.	Auto Maint.	Insur-ance	Clothes	Medical

FORM 6

SAVINGS ACCOUNT ALLOCATIONS

Date	Deposit	With-drawal	Balance	Housing	Food	Auto Insur.	Auto Maint.	Insur-ance	Clothes	Medical				

FORM 6

SAVINGS ACCOUNT ALLOCATIONS

Date	Deposit	With-drawal	Balance	Housing	Food	Auto Insur.	Auto Maint.	Insur-ance	Clothes	Medical

FORM 6

INDIVIDUAL ACCOUNT PAGE

ACCOUNT CATEGORY	$ _____ ALLOCATION	$ _____ ALLOCATION

DATE	TRANSACTION	DEPOSIT	WITHDRAWAL	BALANCE

FORM 7

INDIVIDUAL ACCOUNT PAGE

_____ $ _____ $ _____
ACCOUNT CATEGORY   ALLOCATION   ALLOCATION

DATE	TRANSACTION	DEPOSIT	WITHDRAWAL	BALANCE

FORM 7

INDIVIDUAL ACCOUNT PAGE

	$		$	
ACCOUNT CATEGORY	ALLOCATION		ALLOCATION	

DATE	TRANSACTION	DEPOSIT	WITHDRAWAL	BALANCE

FORM 7

INDIVIDUAL ACCOUNT PAGE

	$		$	
ACCOUNT CATEGORY	ALLOCATION		ALLOCATION	

DATE	TRANSACTION	DEPOSIT	WITHDRAWAL	BALANCE

FORM 7

INDIVIDUAL ACCOUNT PAGE

_____ $ _____ $ _____
ACCOUNT CATEGORY   ALLOCATION   ALLOCATION

DATE	TRANSACTION	DEPOSIT	WITHDRAWAL	BALANCE

FORM 7

INDIVIDUAL ACCOUNT PAGE

_____ $ _____ $ _____
ACCOUNT CATEGORY ALLOCATION ALLOCATION

DATE	TRANSACTION	DEPOSIT	WITHDRAWAL	BALANCE

INDIVIDUAL ACCOUNT PAGE

_____ $ _____ $ _____
ACCOUNT CATEGORY   ALLOCATION   ALLOCATION

DATE	TRANSACTION	DEPOSIT	WITHDRAWAL	BALANCE

FORM 7

INDIVIDUAL ACCOUNT PAGE

_____ $ _____ $ _____
ACCOUNT CATEGORY   ALLOCATION   ALLOCATION

DATE	TRANSACTION	DEPOSIT	WITHDRAWAL	BALANCE

FORM 7

INDIVIDUAL ACCOUNT PAGE

	$		$	
ACCOUNT CATEGORY	ALLOCATION		ALLOCATION	

DATE	TRANSACTION	DEPOSIT	WITHDRAWAL	BALANCE

FORM 7

INDIVIDUAL ACCOUNT PAGE

_____ $ _____ $ _____
ACCOUNT CATEGORY   ALLOCATION   ALLOCATION

DATE	TRANSACTION	DEPOSIT	WITHDRAWAL	BALANCE

FORM 7

INDIVIDUAL ACCOUNT PAGE

_____ $ _____ $ _____
ACCOUNT CATEGORY   ALLOCATION   ALLOCATION

DATE	TRANSACTION	DEPOSIT	WITHDRAWAL	BALANCE

FORM 7

INDIVIDUAL ACCOUNT PAGE

$ _____ $ _____

ACCOUNT CATEGORY   ALLOCATION   ALLOCATION

DATE	TRANSACTION	DEPOSIT	WITHDRAWAL	BALANCE	

FORM 7

INDIVIDUAL ACCOUNT PAGE

_____ $ _____ $ _____

ACCOUNT CATEGORY   ALLOCATION   ALLOCATION

DATE	TRANSACTION	DEPOSIT	WITHDRAWAL	BALANCE

FORM 7

INDIVIDUAL ACCOUNT PAGE

_____ $ _____ $ _____
ACCOUNT CATEGORY   ALLOCATION   ALLOCATION

DATE	TRANSACTION	DEPOSIT	WITHDRAWAL	BALANCE

FORM 7

INDIVIDUAL ACCOUNT PAGE

_____ $ _____ $ _____
ACCOUNT CATEGORY   ALLOCATION   ALLOCATION

DATE	TRANSACTION	DEPOSIT	WITHDRAWAL	BALANCE	

FORM 7

INDIVIDUAL ACCOUNT PAGE

_____ $ _____ $ _____
ACCOUNT CATEGORY   ALLOCATION   ALLOCATION

DATE	TRANSACTION	DEPOSIT	WITHDRAWAL	BALANCE

FORM 7

INDIVIDUAL ACCOUNT PAGE

DATE	TRANSACTION	DEPOSIT	WITHDRAWAL	BALANCE

FORM 7

INDIVIDUAL ACCOUNT PAGE

_____ $ _____ $ _____
ACCOUNT CATEGORY   ALLOCATION   ALLOCATION

DATE	TRANSACTION	DEPOSIT	WITHDRAWAL	BALANCE

FORM 7

INDIVIDUAL ACCOUNT PAGE

$ _____ $ _____

_____   ALLOCATION   ALLOCATION
ACCOUNT CATEGORY

DATE	TRANSACTION	DEPOSIT	WITHDRAWAL	BALANCE

INDIVIDUAL ACCOUNT PAGE

		$ _____		$ _____	
ACCOUNT CATEGORY		ALLOCATION		ALLOCATION	

DATE	TRANSACTION	DEPOSIT	WITHDRAWAL	BALANCE

FORM 7

INDIVIDUAL ACCOUNT PAGE

	$		$	
ACCOUNT CATEGORY		ALLOCATION		ALLOCATION

DATE	TRANSACTION	DEPOSIT	WITHDRAWAL	BALANCE

FORM 7

INDIVIDUAL ACCOUNT PAGE

		$		$	
	ACCOUNT CATEGORY	ALLOCATION		ALLOCATION	

DATE	TRANSACTION	DEPOSIT	WITHDRAWAL	BALANCE

FORM 7

INDIVIDUAL ACCOUNT PAGE

$ _____ $ _____

_____ ACCOUNT CATEGORY   ALLOCATION   ALLOCATION

DATE	TRANSACTION	DEPOSIT	WITHDRAWAL	BALANCE

FORM 7

INDIVIDUAL ACCOUNT PAGE

_____ $ _____ $ _____
ACCOUNT CATEGORY   ALLOCATION   ALLOCATION

DATE	TRANSACTION	DEPOSIT	WITHDRAWAL	BALANCE

FORM 7

INDIVIDUAL ACCOUNT PAGE

ACCOUNT CATEGORY	$ ALLOCATION	$ ALLOCATION

DATE	TRANSACTION	DEPOSIT	WITHDRAWAL	BALANCE

INDIVIDUAL ACCOUNT PAGE

_____ $ _____ $ _____
ACCOUNT CATEGORY   ALLOCATION   ALLOCATION

DATE	TRANSACTION	DEPOSIT		WITHDRAWAL		BALANCE	

FORM 7

INDIVIDUAL ACCOUNT PAGE

	$ _____	$ _____
ACCOUNT CATEGORY	ALLOCATION	ALLOCATION

DATE	TRANSACTION	DEPOSIT	WITHDRAWAL	BALANCE

INDIVIDUAL ACCOUNT PAGE

_____ $ _____ $ _____
ACCOUNT CATEGORY   ALLOCATION   ALLOCATION

DATE	TRANSACTION	DEPOSIT		WITHDRAWAL		BALANCE	

INDIVIDUAL ACCOUNT PAGE

_____ $ _____ $ _____
ACCOUNT CATEGORY   ALLOCATION   ALLOCATION

DATE	TRANSACTION	DEPOSIT	WITHDRAWAL	BALANCE

INDIVIDUAL ACCOUNT PAGE

ACCOUNT CATEGORY $ _____ ALLOCATION $ _____ ALLOCATION

DATE	TRANSACTION	DEPOSIT		WITHDRAWAL		BALANCE	

FORM 7

INDIVIDUAL ACCOUNT PAGE

	$		$	
ACCOUNT CATEGORY	ALLOCATION		ALLOCATION	

DATE	TRANSACTION	DEPOSIT	WITHDRAWAL	BALANCE

FORM 7

INDIVIDUAL ACCOUNT PAGE

$ _____ $ _____

_____   ALLOCATION   ALLOCATION
ACCOUNT CATEGORY

DATE	TRANSACTION	DEPOSIT		WITHDRAWAL		BALANCE	

FORM 7

INDIVIDUAL ACCOUNT PAGE

		$ _____		$ _____	
ACCOUNT CATEGORY		ALLOCATION		ALLOCATION	

DATE	TRANSACTION	DEPOSIT	WITHDRAWAL	BALANCE

FORM 7

INDIVIDUAL ACCOUNT PAGE

	$		$	
ACCOUNT CATEGORY		ALLOCATION		ALLOCATION

DATE	TRANSACTION	DEPOSIT	WITHDRAWAL	BALANCE

FORM 7

CHECKBOOK LEDGER

DATE	CK. #	TRANSACTION	DEPOSIT	WITHDRAWAL	BALANCE

FORM 7a

CHECKBOOK LEDGER

DATE	CK. #	TRANSACTION	DEPOSIT	WITHDRAWAL	BALANCE

FORM 7a

CHECKBOOK LEDGER

DATE	CK. #	TRANSACTION	DEPOSIT	WITHDRAWAL	BALANCE

FORM 7a

CHECKBOOK LEDGER

DATE	CK. #	TRANSACTION	DEPOSIT	WITHDRAWAL	BALANCE

FORM 7a

CHECKBOOK LEDGER

DATE	CK. #	TRANSACTION	DEPOSIT	WITHDRAWAL	BALANCE

CHECKBOOK LEDGER

DATE	CK. #	TRANSACTION	DEPOSIT	WITHDRAWAL	BALANCE

FORM 7a

CHECKBOOK LEDGER

DATE	CK. #	TRANSACTION	DEPOSIT	WITHDRAWAL	BALANCE

FORM 7a

CHECKBOOK LEDGER

DATE	CK. #	TRANSACTION	DEPOSIT	WITHDRAWAL	BALANCE

FORM 7a

CHECKBOOK LEDGER

DATE	CK. #	TRANSACTION	DEPOSIT	WITHDRAWAL	BALANCE

FORM 7a

CHECKBOOK LEDGER

DATE	CK. #	TRANSACTION	DEPOSIT	WITHDRAWAL	BALANCE

FORM 7a

CHECKBOOK LEDGER

DATE	CK. #	TRANSACTION	DEPOSIT	WITHDRAWAL	BALANCE

FORM 7a

CHECKBOOK LEDGER

DATE	CK. #	TRANSACTION	DEPOSIT	WITHDRAWAL	BALANCE

FORM 7a

CHECKBOOK LEDGER

DATE	CK. #	TRANSACTION	DEPOSIT	WITHDRAWAL	BALANCE

FORM 7a

CHECKBOOK LEDGER

DATE	CK. #	TRANSACTION	DEPOSIT	WITHDRAWAL	BALANCE

FORM 7a

CHECKBOOK LEDGER

DATE	CK. #	TRANSACTION	DEPOSIT	WITHDRAWAL	BALANCE

CHECKBOOK LEDGER

DATE	CK. #	TRANSACTION	DEPOSIT	WITHDRAWAL	BALANCE

FORM 7a

LIST OF DEBTS

as of _____

TO WHOM OWED	CONTACT NAME PHONE NO.	PAY OFF	PAYMENTS LEFT	MONTHLY PAYMENT	DUE DATE

FORM 8

LIST OF DEBTS

as of _____

TO WHOM OWED	CONTACT NAME / PHONE NO.	PAY OFF	PAYMENTS LEFT	MONTHLY PAYMENT	DUE DATE

FORM 8

LIST OF DEBTS
as of _____

TO WHOM OWED	CONTACT NAME PHONE NO.	PAY OFF	PAYMENTS LEFT	MONTHLY PAYMENT	DUE DATE

FORM 8

LIST OF DEBTS

as of _____

TO WHOM OWED	CONTACT NAME PHONE NO.	PAY OFF	PAYMENTS LEFT	MONTHLY PAYMENT	DUE DATE

FORM 8

INDIVIDUAL ACCOUNT PAGE

_____ $ _____ $ _____

ACCOUNT CATEGORY   ALLOCATION   ALLOCATION

DATE	TRANSACTION	DEPOSIT	WITHDRAWAL	BALANCE

FORM 7

CHECKBOOK LEDGER

DATE	CK. #	TRANSACTION	DEPOSIT	WITHDRAWAL	BALANCE

FORM 7a